Delightful *Quilts* in *Bloom*

Mary Ross
& Barbara Scheu

The American Quilter's Society (AQS), located in Paducah, Kentucky, is dedicated to promoting the accomplishments of today's quilters. Through its publications and events, AQS strives to honor today's quiltmakers and their work and to inspire future creativity and innovation in quiltmaking.

Text © 2008, Authors, Mary Ross & Barbara Scheu
Artwork © 2008 American Quilter's Society

Executive Editor: Nicole C. Chambers
Editor: Linda Baxter Lasco
Graphic Design: Brent Andrew
Cover Design: Michael Buckingham
Photography: Charles R. Lynch

Special thanks to Caryl Bryer Fallert of Bryerpatch Studio in Paducah's LowerTown Arts District for the use of her home for our location photographs.

American Quilter's Society
P. O. Box 3290 • Paducah, KY 42002-3290 • PHONE: (270) 898-7903 • FAX: (270) 898-1173
w w w . a m e r i c a n q u i l t e r . c o m

Additional copies of this book may be ordered from the American Quilter's Society, PO Box 3290, Paducah, KY 42002-3290, or online at: www.AmericanQuilter.com.

Library of Congress Cataloging-in-Publication Data

Ross, Mary, 1939-
  Delightful quilts in bloom / by Mary Ross & Barbara Scheu.
      p. cm
  Summary: "Instructions on appliqué basics and no-fail miter technique. Patterns for a full-sized, twelve-block quilt that is easy enough for a novice yet appealing to an expert. Smaller projects include a pillowcase, pillows, table runners, and wallhangings. Lattice sashing instructions and a meandering vine border design included"--Provided by publisher.
  ISBN 978-1-57432-949-0
  1. Quilting. 2. Quilting--Patterns. I. Scheu, Barbara. II. Title.
  TT835.R675 2008
  746.46'041--dc22

                              2008000944

Proudly printed and bound in the United States of America.

Acknowledgments

When we started designing the first block for our featured quilt and presented it to our guild, the interest in this block-of-the-month project was overwhelming. Our friend Susana Farrier had already planted the idea for us to publish our patterns. When Bobbie Aug, appraiser, quilter, and author, gave us encouragement and direction for writing a book, we began the process of being published. AQS has made the possibility become a reality.

We realized right away that we needed to hold monthly meetings to glean inspiration from one another. Our appliqué group tested our patterns and gave us invaluable advice and support. Our friendships blossomed while working together and sharing with one another at these meetings—thus, the name of the featured quilt, BLOSSOMS OF FRIENDSHIP.

The following months were filled with more designs, quilting, and many long hours of writing and editing. We could not have met the goals without the help and encouragement of our AQS editor, Nicole Chambers, Bobbie Aug, and our dear husbands, who were faithful in helping us maintain our home life while giving extra help and advice. Pete, Mary's husband, is the computer expert who kept the writing going smoothly. Jim, Barbara's husband, made sure she continued her exercise program, artwork, and reminded her to call family and friends.

Made by Ludene Smith and machine quilted by Joyce Schiltz, both of Montrose, Colorado

3

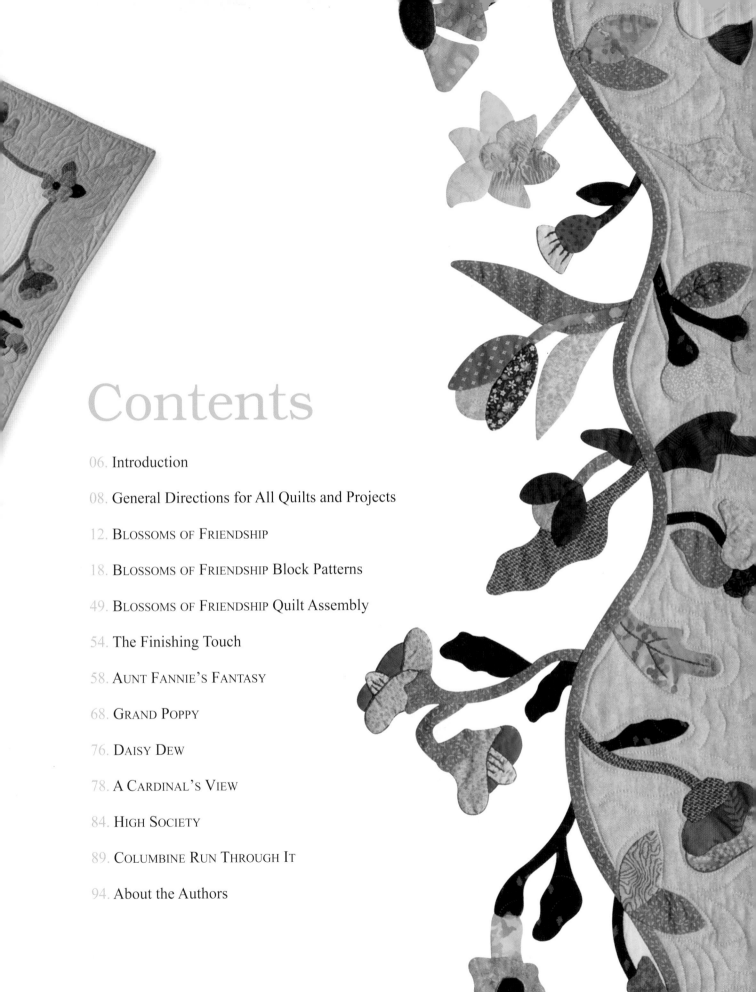

Contents

Introduction

Mary and Barb

Just as the arrival of spring chases away our winter blues with the promise of flowers, so does making a floral appliqué quilt. It reminds us of our family and childhood home where there was always a row of beautiful flowers growing in the garden.

We will always love the traditional quilts that Grandma appliquéd and pieced. We are grateful for the quilting heritage that has been passed down to us through these creative pioneers. Our designs reflect that heritage and our past family histories. We hope you will enjoy the stories, artwork, and quilt patterns contained herein as much as we enjoyed designing and writing about them.

Our quilts and projects are for any level of quilter, with the exception of the border on BLOSSOMS OF FRIENDSHIP. It is perhaps more appropriate for the intermediate or advanced appliqué artist.

From Mary

The Friendship Quilters of Western Colorado, our local quilt guild, asked me to create an appliqué block-of-the-month pattern. I felt that I needed some assistance and called my artist friend Barb to see if she would team up with me on the project.

From Barb

I agreed. I'm a novice quilter, but we found combining our skills and talents to be fun and productive. I'd design feathery flowers and Mary would transform them into pieces suitable for appliqué. She'd then draft a new pattern and I'd show her how to blend the pattern to improve the flow.

From Mary and Barb

We learned a lot from each other and hope that you will now enjoy the fruits of our labor by reading this book and making the quilts and various projects.

We challenge you to form an appliqué block-of-the-month group. Our group has had so much fun. We really enjoyed showing our completed work at each meeting. It is a great way to form lasting friendships and to have an heirloom quilt for your family.

The Appliqué Group

Left to right from the bottom: Lida Letey, Ludene Smith, Leah Morgan, Carole Peterson, Shirley Hast, Barbara Scheu, Nancy Moore, Frances Ruckman, Sue Peters, Debbie Miles, Mary Ross, Sue Sharman, Sue Hillhouse. Carolyn Casedy

The BLOSSOMS OF FRIENDSHIP quilt is suitable for a monthly or bimonthly project. Many of our ladies enjoy a more leisurely pace, with time to work on other projects while still able to meet the group goals.

The monthly meeting is a great place to work on problem solving, teaching techniques, or just enjoy a cup of tea with friends.

General Directions for All Quilts and Projects

Fabric Preparation

Wash and press your fabrics to remove excess dye and prevent shrinkage later. Clipping an inch off the corners at a 45-degree angle will prevent excessive unraveling. Use the type of soap that you will be using to care for your finished quilt. Check with your local quilt shop for a product that is safe to use on quilts. After laundering, remove the selvages.

Fabric Selection

You will need a wide variety of green fabrics for appliqué leaves and stems. Start with greens that you may already have in your stash of fabrics and add more as needed. The variety of shades and scale of prints will add charm and interest to your quilt. Include a variety of fabric prints for flowers, birds, butterflies, and dragonflies.

Try to have at least three values in every color that you will be using. Having five to eight is even better. Choose a variety of scales, from small- to medium-sized prints. Choose three to five large prints for fussy cutting petals, birds, and butterflies. Scraps, sweet 16s (half of a fat eighth), eighth- and quarter-yard cuts (fat or off the bolt) will be sufficient for most of your fabrics. Buy up to one-half yard of the large-scale prints. Your appliqué will be enhanced by a great variety of prints.

Your fabrics should combine to set the mood, whether country, Victorian, '30s, '80s, reproductions, Amish solids, etc. You can choose a monochromatic palette for each block or use the scrappy look of our quilts. Choose an appropriate color scheme based upon where the quilt will be used or who will be receiving it.

For a scrap quilt, use each fabric in at least three or four of your blocks. Remember to set aside some of the block fabrics to use in an appliquéd border.

Thread

The best thread to use for appliqué is a 60- or 50-weight 100 percent cotton or silk. Select threads that match the appliqué piece, not the background. Cut your thread no longer than 14" to prevent knotting and fraying. Silk thread comes in many neutral shades that blend well with the color of your appliqué.

Seam Allowance

We recommend a ³⁄₁₆" seam allowance for appliqué. All pieced seams in the quilts are ¼" unless otherwise stated.

Bias Stems

Cut bias strips three times the desired finished width of the stem. Dampen the fabric and press ⅓ of the width lengthwise toward the wrong side of the fabric, using a **dry iron**. (You will burn your fingers if you use steam.) Turn and press the remaining long side just until it meets the fold you just pressed. This will make a tri-fold bias stem. For example, a ¾" wide strip will finish into a ¼" stem.

1st fold

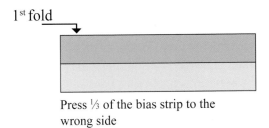

Press ⅓ of the bias strip to the wrong side

2nd fold

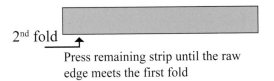

Press remaining strip until the raw edge meets the first fold

Circles

Using a drafting circle template, which can be found at office supply and variety stores, draw a circle onto firm, heat-resistant template plastic, the finished size of the desired circle. Cut this out carefully and remove any rough burrs with an emery board, being careful not to distort the circle.

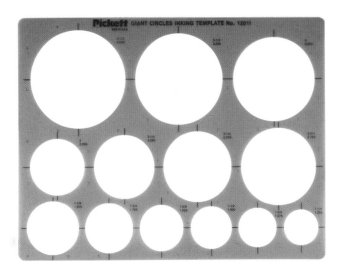

Tip: *If you do not have heat-resistant template plastic, try layering about three pieces of freezer-paper circles ironed together.*

Using the circle template again, find a circle that is ¼" to ⅜" larger than the desired finished size and draw the larger circle on the wrong side of your selected fabric. Cut the fabric circle out on the drawn line. Sew this circle with a small basting stitch ⅛" inside the raw edge, beginning with a knot on the right side of the fabric. Place your template in the center of the wrong side of the fabric and pull the basting thread to draw up the edges. Space the gathers evenly.

Turn the circle over and be sure the fabric is smooth and just the way you want it to look on your block. While holding the thread taut, dampen or use steam and press the circle from the top. Allow this to dry on the ironing board. When dry, remove the template, like unbuttoning a shirt, and save it to use on the next circle of that size. If the circle is misshapen, draw the thread gently until the fabric is smooth again and re-press. Cut the thread tail and knot off just before appliquéing. You do not need to remove the basting.

Yo-Yos

Using a circle template, draw and cut out a circle two times larger than the finished size that you desire. Fold the raw edge of the circle under 3/16" to the wrong side and take small running stitches around the circle. Use a strong thread that will hold the gathers. Draw the circle up as tight as the center allows and tack in place. Press flat with the opening in the center of the yo-yo. Yo-yos can be appliquéd either smooth or open side up.

Applique

Although this book is not intended to teach you how to appliqué, we have included instructions for the freezer-paper-on-the-underside method. However, the patterns are all adaptable to the method of your choice.

Getting Started

✓ Enlarge your pattern to the correct size. Make a tracing paper pattern of the design including the dashed center lines. When you layer the appliqué and your marked lines are covered, this will help to align the topmost pieces.

Fold the background fabric in half horizontally and press. Unfold, refold vertically, and press again. These folds will align with the center lines on the appliqué pattern.

Using a light box or glass pane with a light shining through from underneath, secure the pattern, **right-side up**, over the glass. Place the background fabric,

right-side up, squarely on top, aligning the center folds and center lines, and tape it in place. Trace the pattern onto the right side of your fabric background, **just inside the pattern line,** with a fine line .05 mm mechanical pencil to ensure that the appliqué will cover the drawn lines. Do **not** mark the individual pattern numbers or the center alignment dashes on your fabric.

Remove the background fabric. Turn the pattern over so it is **wrong-side up** on the light box. Place a sheet of freezer paper with the wax-side down over the wrong side of the pattern and trace each piece just **outside the pattern line.** Mark each piece with the pattern number. Accurately cut the pieces out on the drawn line and place in a plastic zip-close bag until ready for use.

Tip: Trace each piece individually, as the patterns are not symmetrical and each flower is a bit different, even though they may look the same. This will ensure the right fit as you sew.

Select the fabric for each pattern piece and iron the freezer-paper pattern, wax-side down, onto the wrong side of the fabric. Use a dry, hot iron and press for two to three seconds. Allow a few seconds to cool and then cut out the fabric **adding a 3/16" seam allowance on all sides.** Leave a slightly larger seam allowance on any side that tucks under another piece.

Stack the pieces in the order of appliqué or pin them on the pattern in their approximate position until ready for use. You will be removing them one piece at a time to place on your block and this will keep them out of the way while you are sewing.

Before appliquéing, clip any inside (concave) curves by making three snips halfway through the seam allowance. On a long gentle curve, take more snips about 1/4" apart.

We recommend that you take an appliqué class at your local shop or have a friend work with you to help perfect your stitch and learn to do points and curves. We rounded points and smoothed curves to make them easy for you.

Removing the Freezer Paper

After you have aligned, pinned, and begun sewing, keep in mind that the freezer paper must be removed.

Most appliqué pieces tuck under other pieces, so you can appliqué several sides and remove the paper through the opening. Using pointed tweezers, loosen the freezer paper and pull it out. Other pieces that are sewn all around or that get too narrow to remove the paper must have the paper removed before you finish sewing. To do this, crease the fabric against the paper in the unsewn area and remove the paper. Refold on the crease and complete the appliqué.

Appliqué by Number

In all quilts, you will begin with piece number 1 and appliqué to the highest number. Concentrate on one piece at a time and before you know it, you will be finished. Follow the appliqué sequence listed on each pattern. It is as easy as 1, 2, 3!

Pressing

When your appliqué is complete, place it face down on a thick terry towel and press from the wrong side. Then center your pattern and trim the completed piece to the correct size.

Optional Embellishment and Embroidery

The lines for butterfly antennae, flower stamens, veins on leaves, etc., are for embroidery, embellishment, or quilting.

Use a small black seed bead or embroider French knots for the eyes of the birds, butterflies, and dragonflies.

Machine embroidery can also be used, as we did on the table runner.

Helpful Hints

Take a stitch in the background fabric well under the piece to be appliquéd, coming up in the fold where you want to begin stitching. This will keep the thread tail out of the way.

When you insert your needle down to take a stitch, be sure you enter the background fabric behind where your thread just came out of the fold. This will shorten your stitches and make a tight seam.

When you reach a point, take two stitches close together. Lift the appliqué piece up and trim a little of the seam allowance that you just tucked under. This will allow more room for the seam that you are getting ready to turn under. Use a round wooden toothpick, lightly moistened on the end, to tuck the second side of the point under. Turning with the needle sometimes pulls the fabric back out, but the toothpick seems to hold the fabric in. Before you begin sewing the next side, take a small tug on your thread to pull the point back out.

Keep several needles loaded with your most frequently used colors of threads, cut approximately 14" long.

Fold the seam allowance under and crease against the freezer paper on each side that you will be appliquéing. This gives you a sewing guide, even if the paper loosens, as cotton has a memory and will hold the crease.

BLOSSOMS of FRIENDSHIP

BLOSSOMS OF FRIENDSHIP is easier to make than it looks. We have rounded or widened the points to make room for turning under the seam allowances. We have also widened the concave curves. You should never have to clip into the curves more than ⅔ of the seam allowance. Just as my husband often quotes, "You climb a mountain one step at a time," so will you add one piece at a time and attain your goal.

Let's Get Started!

Begin by reading all the **General Directions for All Quilts and Projects, pages 8–11.**

Plan ahead to have enough fabric for matching pillows and/or pillowcases by adding to the yardage for this quilt.

Yardage

Fabric A ~ 6¼ yards
> *Includes blocks, inside sashing, inside border, and cornerstones*

Fabric B ~ 4¾ yards
> *Includes outside border, sashing, and cornerstones*

Fabric C ~ 1¼ yards
> *Seamless border vine*

BLOSSOMS OF FRIENDSHIP

Quilt size: 82" x 101". Finished block size: 16" x 16".
Made by Barbara Scheu and machine quilted by
Laurie Gerse, both of Montrose, Colorado.

Mary Ross & Barbara Scheu ~ Delightful Quilts in Bloom

Yardage continued

Baskets

    scraps or fat quarters equalling a total of 1½ yards

    Note: *The Miss Zinnia block will require a fat quarter all to itself*

Stems and leaves ~ 3½ yards

    a variety of different size prints, values, and textures

Flowers, birds, butterflies, and dragonflies

    scraps and small yardages in a variety of colors and values 4½ yards total

Binding ~ ¾ yard

Backing ~ 8½ yards

Queen-size batting ~ 90" x 108"

Cutting

Cut in the order given. Be sure to cut the border pieces on the lengthwise grain of fabric.

Fabric A
Inside border
    2 strips 7½" x 108"
    2 strips 7 ½" x 90"
    For solid block variation
    12 squares 17½" x 17½"

DO NOT CUT strips across the fabric width and then cut squares. You will need the extra fabric beyond the squares to cut the sashing strips. Use the remaining yardage to cut all the sashing strips and cornerstone triangles.

Inside sashing strips
    31 strips 2" x 16½"

Cornerstones
    2 squares 4" x 4" cut once on the diagonal

    18 squares 3⅛" x 3⅛" cut twice on the diagonal

Fabric B

Outside border
2 strips 7½" x 108"
2 strips 7½" x 90"

Outside sashing strips
62 strips 1½" x 16½"

Cornerstones
20 rectangles 1⅞" x 6"
36 rectangles 1⅞" x 2¾"

Bias Vine for Appliqué Border

Fold the 1¼ yards of vine fabric on the diagonal to form a 45-degree angle and cut on the fold. Cut a total of eight strips of 1⅛" wide bias. You will need the four longest strips for the side borders and the four shorter strips for the top and bottom borders. By cutting from this center fold, you will not have to piece the vine. One end of each bias strip will fit under the border center flower and the other under the border corner flower.

Four-Patch Background

Optional: cut 48 squares, 9"x 9" from a variety of fabric. Select four different squares and join them into a four-patch unit for the block background. Make 12.

When placing the appliqué, line up the seams in the background with the vertical and horizontal center lines of each pattern.

Making the Quilt

See the General Directions for Appliqué on pages 10–11 for alignment and pattern-transfer instructions.

Appliqué Sequence

Pattern pieces are identified with letter/number combinations. Appliqué all the numbered A pieces in numerical order before beginning the B pieces. The border will have a few C pieces to add after it is attached to the quilt top.

BLOSSOMS OF FRIENDSHIP

Quilt size: 82" x 101". Finished block size: 16" x 16".
Made and hand quilted by
Mary Ross of Montrose, Colorado.

Mary Ross & Barbara Scheu ~ Delightful Quilts in Bloom

BLOSSOMS OF FRIENDSHIP
Block Patterns

Miss Daisy

Miss Pansy

Miss Ginny

Miss Daphne

Miss Collette

Miss Lily

Miss Poppy

Miss Susana

Miss Rose

Miss Belle

Miss Zinnia

Miss Iris

Mary Ross & Barbara Scheu ~ Delightful Quilts in Bloom

Miss Daisy
Finished block size: 16"x16"

▴ *Mary's Four-Patch background*
Refer to the General Directions,
pages 8–11

◂ *Barbara's solid background*

Mary Ross & Barbara Scheu ~ Delightful Quilts in Bloom

Appliqué sequence:

- A1–A72
- B1–B10

Enlarge Illustration by 200%

Miss Pansy

Finished block size: 16"x16"

▲ **Mary's Four-Patch background**
 Refer to the General Directions,
 pages 8–11

◂ **Barbara's solid background**

Mary Ross & Barbara Scheu ~ Delightful Quilts in Bloom

Appliqué sequence:

- A1–A50
- B1–B2
- Tuck B3 under B4
- B4–B6
- Complete B3
- B7–B17

Enlarge Illustration by 200%

Miss Ginny
Finished block size: 16"x16"

▲ **Mary's Four-Patch background**
Refer to the General Directions,
pages 8–11

◄ **Barbara's solid background**

Appliqué sequence:

- A1–A41
- A42 Leave open between asterisks
- A 43–A48
- B1–B13
- Complete A42
- B14–B18

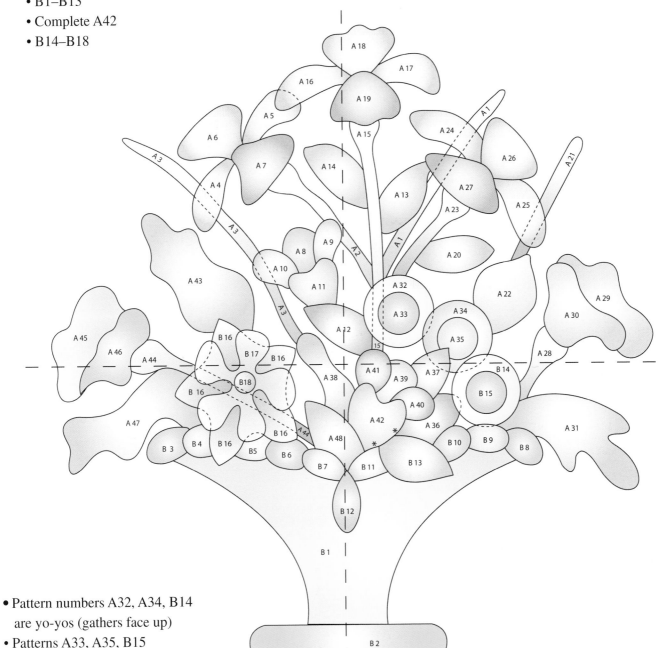

- Pattern numbers A32, A34, B14 are yo-yos (gathers face up)
- Patterns A33, A35, B15 are yo-yos (gathers down)

See yo-yo directions on page 10

Enlarge Illustration by 200%

Miss Daphne
Finished block size: 16"x16"

▲ **Mary's Four-Patch background**
Refer to the General Directions,
pages 8–11

◂ **Barbara's solid background**

Mary Ross & Barbara Scheu ~ Delightful Quilts in Bloom

Appliqué sequence:

- A1–A6
- Tuck A7 under A8
- A8–A10
- Complete A7
- A11–A13
- Tuck A14 under A15
- A15–A16
- Complete A14
- A17–A60
- B1–B16
- Reverse hummingbird motif from MISS SUSANA (page 35)

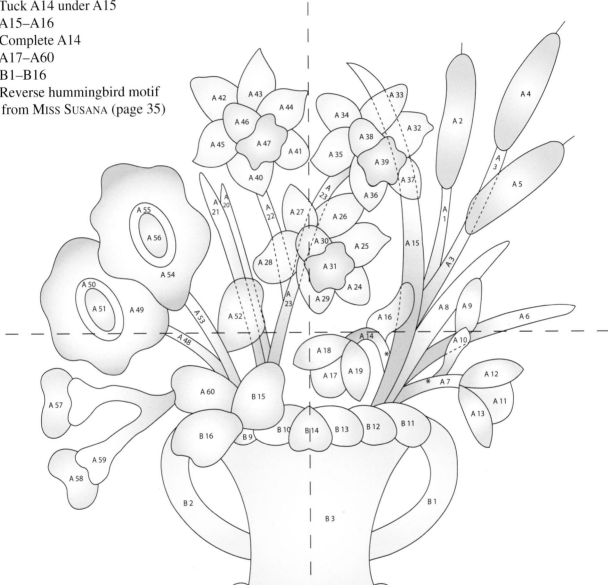

Enlarge Illustration by 200%

Miss Collette

Finished block size: 16"x16"

▴ *Mary's Four-Patch background*
Refer to the General Directions,
pages 8–11

◂ *Barbara's solid background*

Appliqué sequence:

- A1–A11
- A12 Leave open between asterisks
- A13–A72
- Tuck A45 under A46
- To make B1 refer to bottom of page
- B2–B14 refer to bottom of page
- Complete A12

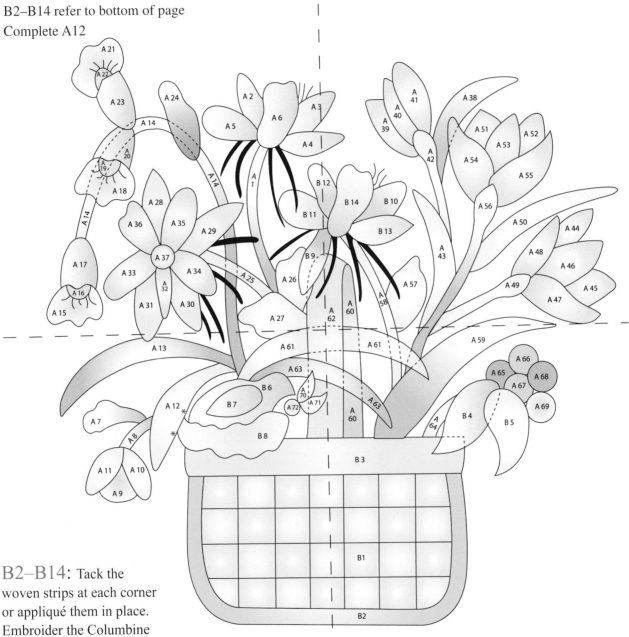

Enlarge Illustration by 200%

B2–B14: Tack the woven strips at each corner or appliqué them in place. Embroider the Columbine tails with three close rows of stem stitches.

B1: To make the woven basket, cut 7 light brown strips 1½" x 3¼" and 4 dark brown strips 1½" x 7". Fold the strips lengthwise, wrong sides together, with the raw edges meeting in the middle of one side. Press and turn smooth side up. Pin the light brown strips vertically to the background, butting them next to each other. Starting at the top of the basket, weave the dark brown strips horizontally. Make sure the ends of the strips will be covered by B2 and B3. Trim where necessary. Baste the woven strips in place.

Miss Lily

Finished block size: 16"x16"

▲ *Mary's Four-Patch background*
Refer to the General Directions,
pages 8–11

◄ *Barbara's solid background*

Mary Ross & Barbara Scheu ~ Delightful Quilts in Bloom

Appliqué sequence:

- A1–A50
- Tuck A51 under A52
- A52
- Tuck A53 under A54
- A54
- Complete A51
- A55
- B1
- Tuck B2 under B3
- B3–B6
- Complete B2
- B7–B19
- Complete A53

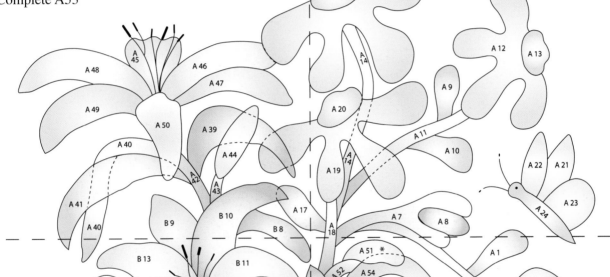
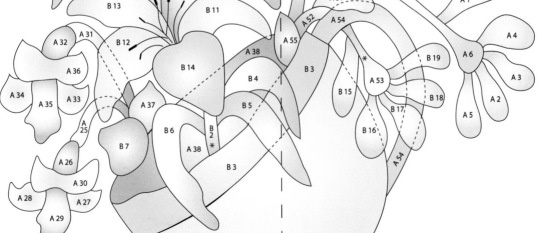

Enlarge Illustration by 200%

Miss Poppy

Finished block size: 16"x16"

▴ **Mary's Four-Patch background**
Refer to the General Directions,
pages 8–11

◂ **Barbara's solid background**

Mary Ross & Barbara Scheu ~ Delightful Quilts in Bloom

Appliqué sequence:

• A1–A58
• B1–B16

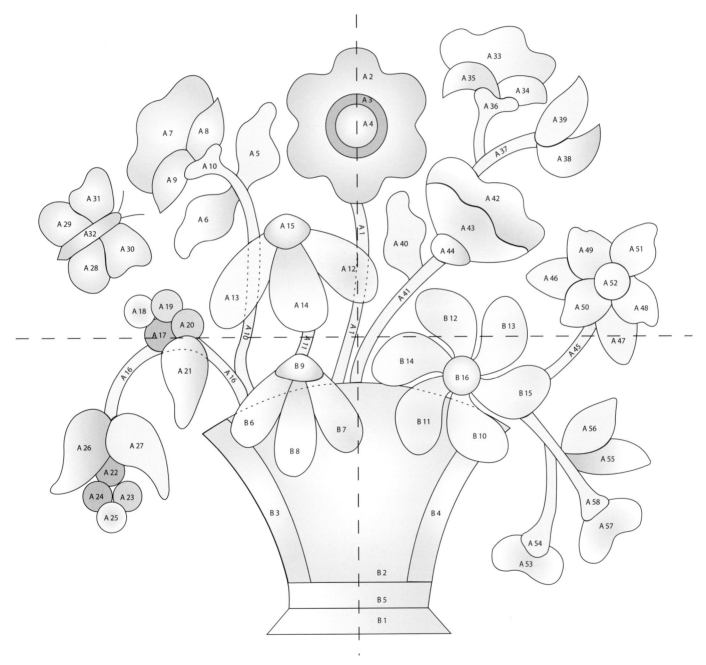

Enlarge Illustration by 200%

Miss Susana

Finished block size: 16"x16"

▲ **Mary's Four-Patch background**
Refer to the General Directions,
pages 8–11

◄ **Barbara's solid background**

Appliqué sequence:

• A1–A20

• Tuck (upper) A24 under A21

• A21–A23

• Complete A24 (Two pieces-upper & lower)

•A25–A58

• B1–B21

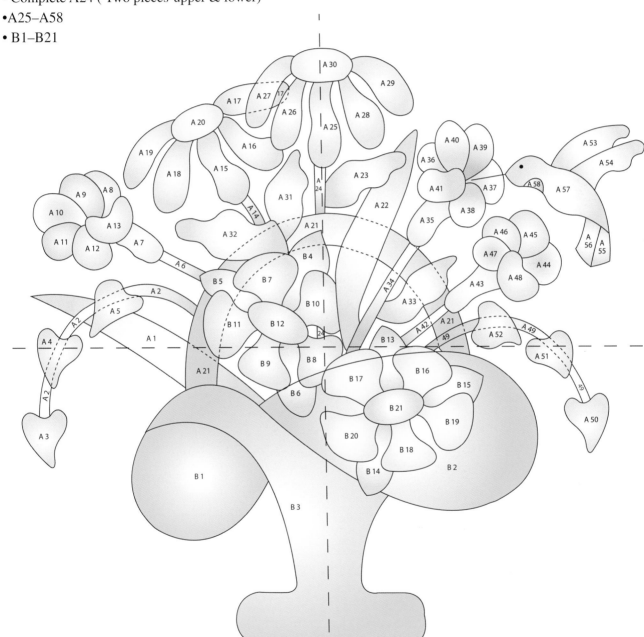

Enlarge Illustration by 200%

Miss Rose

Finished block size: 16"x16"

▲ *Mary's Four-Patch background*
Refer to the General Directions,
pages 8–11

◄ *Barbara's solid background*

Mary Ross & Barbara Scheu ~ Delightful Quilts in Bloom

Appliqué sequence:
- A1–A47
- B1–B23

Enlarge Illustration by 200%

Miss Belle
Finished block size: 16"x16"

▲ *Mary's Four-Patch background*
Refer to the General Directions,
pages 8–11

◄ *Barbara's solid background*

Mary Ross & Barbara Scheu ~ Delightful Quilts in Bloom

Appliqué sequence:

- A1–A44
- Tuck A45 under A46
- A46–A48
- Tuck A49 under A50
- A50–A60
- B1–B5
- Complete A45
- B6–B7
- CompleteA49
- B8–B11

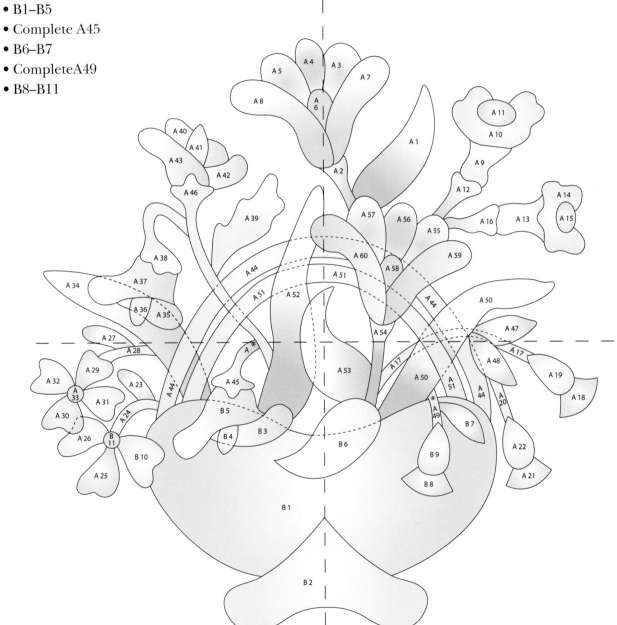

Enlarge Illustration by 200%

Miss Zinnia

Finished block size: 16"x16"

▴*Mary's Four-Patch background*
Refer to the General Directions, pages 8–11

◂ *Barbara's solid background*

Mary Ross & Barbara Scheu ~ Delightful Quilts in Bloom

Appliqué sequence:

- A1–A23
- B1–Leave open between astrerisks
- B2–B8
- Complete B1
- B9-B56

Enlarge Illustration by 200%

Miss Iris

Finished block size: 16"x16"

▴ **Mary's Four-Patch background**
Refer to the General Directions, pages 8–11

◂ **Barbara's solid background**

Mary Ross & Barbara Scheu ~ Delightful Quilts in Bloom

Appliqué sequence:

- A1–A64
- B1–B24

Enlarge Illustration by 200%

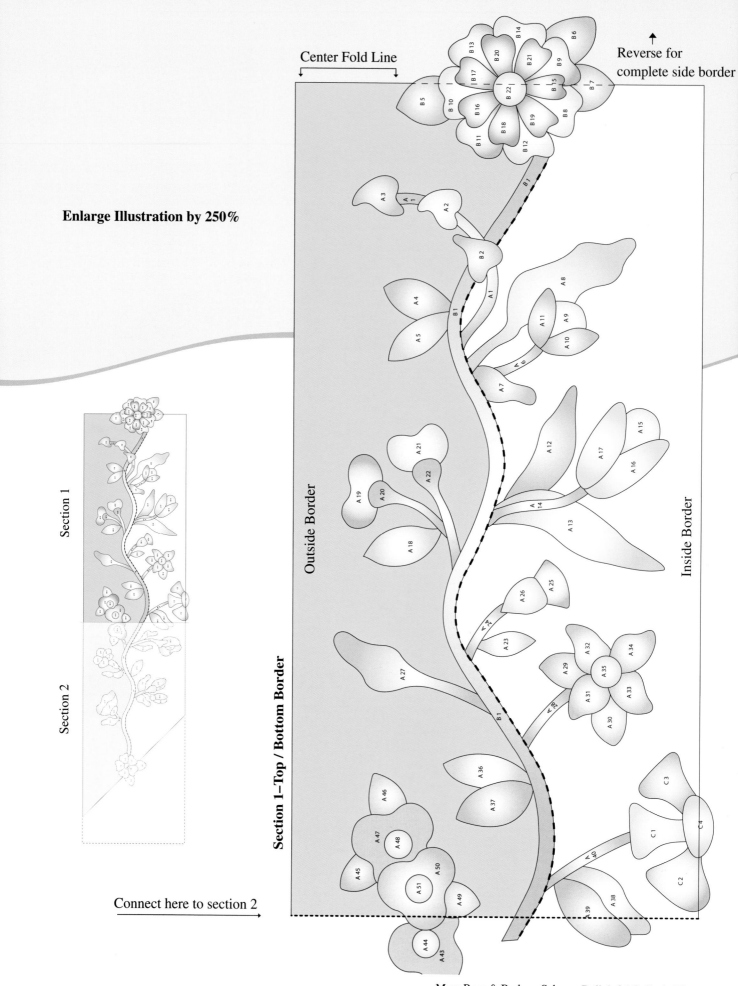

Enlarge Illustration by 250%

Center Fold Line

Reverse for complete side border

Section 1

Section 2

Connect here to section 2

Outside Border

Inside Border

Section 1–Top / Bottom Border

Mary Ross & Barbara Scheu ~ Delightful Quilts in Bloom

44

Enlarge Illustration by 250%

Section 2–Top / Bottom Border

D 2
D 3
D 4
D 1
D 8
D 7
D 5
D 6

A 75
A 76
A 79
A 78
A 77

A 68
A 69
A 67
A 70
A 74
A 72
A 73
A 71

B 1

Inside Border

A 58

B 1

A 59
A 60
A 61
A 66
A 62
A 65
A 63
A 64

Outside Border

A 54
A 55
A 53
A 56
A 57
A 52
A 41
A 42
A 43
A 44

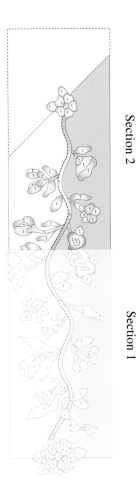

Section 2

Section 1

Connect here to section 1

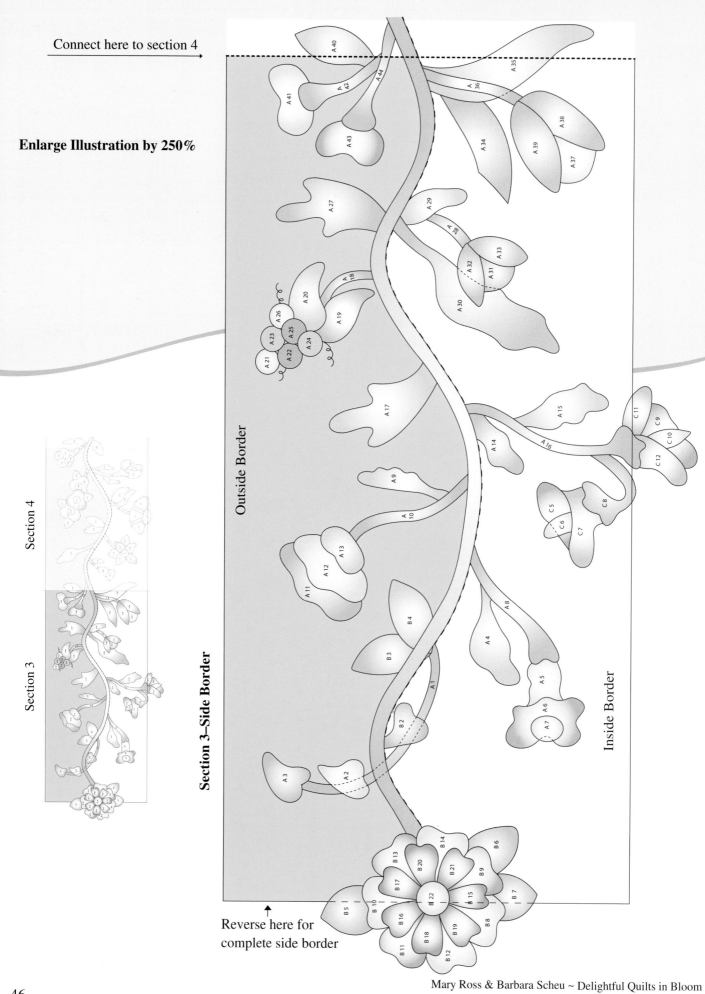

Connect here to section 4

Enlarge Illustration by 250%

Section 4

Section 3

Section 3—Side Border

Outside Border

Inside Border

Reverse here for
complete side border

Mary Ross & Barbara Scheu ~ Delightful Quilts in Bloom

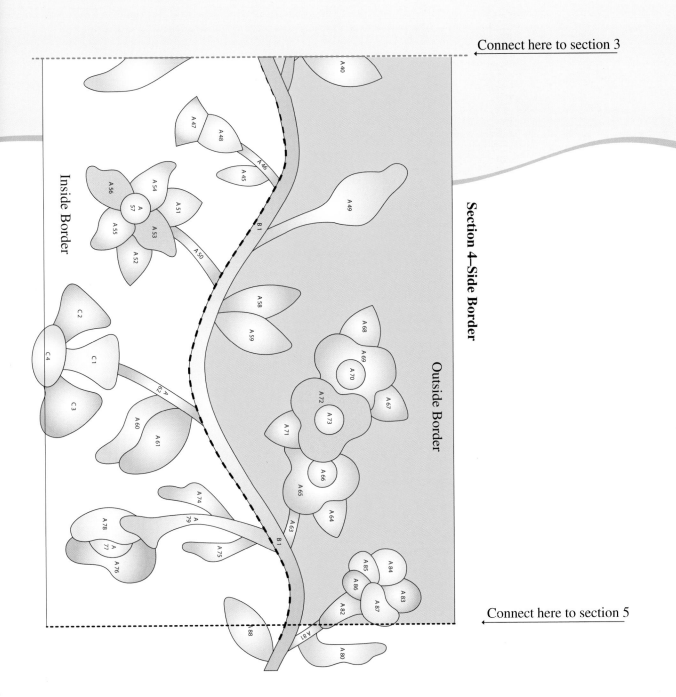

Connect here to section 3

Inside Border

Section 4–Side Border

Outside Border

Connect here to section 5

Enlarge Illustration by 250%

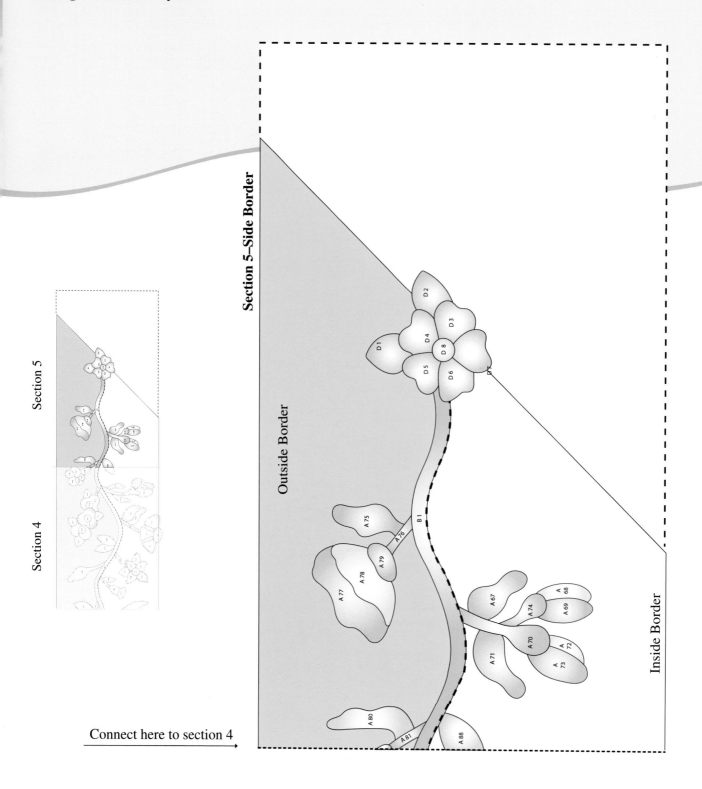

Connect here to section 4 →

See the cutting directions for the lattice-style sashing and the border pieces on pages 15–16. All seam allowances are ¼".

Sashing

Join one 2" x 16½" fabric A sashing strip with two 1½" x 16½" fabric B sashing strips as shown. Press the seam allowances toward fabric B.

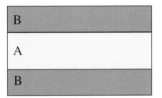

Make 31

Cornerstones

Align the bias edge of a fabric A small triangle along the end of a fabric B small rectangle and sew. Repeat on other side of the rectangle as shown. Make 36 Corner units.

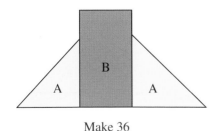

Make 36

Join two corner units to each of 16 fabric B long rectangles as shown. Press the seam allowances toward the long rectangle.

Make 16

Square to 4". Place the corner of a rotary ruler so that the 2" lines intersect the X as shown.

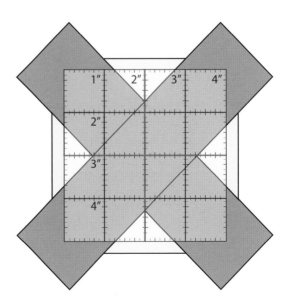

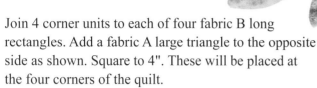

Join 4 corner units to each of four fabric B long rectangles. Add a fabric A large triangle to the opposite side as shown. Square to 4". These will be placed at the four corners of the quilt.

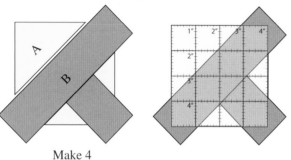

Make 4

Make 3

Assembling Blocks and Sashing

Trim and square each of the appliqué blocks to measure 16½" x 16½". Be sure to keep the baskets level with the bottom of the block.

Lay out the blocks in four rows of three blocks each. Add pieced sashing section to the blocks as shown.

Make 4 rows

Join the blocks and sashing in four horizontal rows. Press the seam allowance toward the sashing.

Make five rows joining cornerstones and sashing strips as shown.

Make 2

Sew the rows of blocks and sashing together.

Option Appliqué some extra birds, butterflies, or dragonflies escaping the blocks into the sashing area.

Appliqué for Borders

For the top and bottom borders, trace sections 1 and 2 (pages 44–45) and tape them together.

For the side borders, trace sections 3–5 (pages 46– 48) and tape them together.

Outside Borders

Cut a 7½" x 45" piece of tracing paper and trace only the dark dashed line from the top and bottom border pattern.

With wrong sides together, press a 7½" x 90" outside border fabric strip in half so it measures 7½" x 54". Lay the pattern on the folded fabric, aligning the edges and the fold lines. Pin the pattern in place. Cut along the drawn curved line through both layers of fabric. **Do not cut the fold** or the **miter seam line.** Repeat for the second 7½" x 90" outside border strip.

Cut a 7½" x 54" piece of tracing paper. Follow the same steps as before, making a tracing paper pattern for the side borders. Fold, press, and cut the 7½" x 108" outside border strips.

On these four **outside** border fabrics draw a pencil line lengthwise on the **wrong side** of the fabric 3½" from the **straight raw edge.**

Piecing the Inside Border to the Outside Border

Place one 7½" x 90" outside curved border, wrong side up. Place one 7½"x 90" inside border strip along that line so it covers the curved edge of the outside border. The entire border should measure 11" wide.

Pin in place and flip over so you now see the curved

line. With your sewing machine on zigzag, stitch the full length on the curved raw edge. Be sure the stitching is less than ¼" wide and is not a tight stitch but rather an elongated zigzag. This stitching will later be covered by a ⅜" vine. It is recommended you use a walking foot here or hand baste these edges with a small running stitch. Keep the edges aligned flat. Do not allow stretching or gathers on these edges. These borders should look like one flat piece of fabric after stitching.

Carefully trim the back of the inside border to within ¼" of the zigzag stitching. Do not get too close to the stitching and break the thread.

Repeat these steps for the other three borders until you have all four inside borders connected to the outside curved borders.

Notice that your borders are longer and wider than you will need for your quilt. Do not trim them yet. We have allowed for fraying edges or any take-up during the appliqué as well as for mitering the corners.

Use the same method of tracing the border pattern on your fabric as you did in your blocks. You will need to reverse the pattern for the opposite end of each border. Do so by turning your tracing paper over and tracing the pieces from the back side.

Appliqué the border, except for the C patterns that extend into the body of the quilt. The vine should just cover the raw edge beyond the zigzag stitching. Stop stitching two inches from the miter seam. Leave the tail of the vine hanging free. You will finish attaching it when the border corners are mitered.

Adding the Border to the Quilt

Your border was made 11" wide to allow for shrinkage. Trim the border to 10½", taking an equal amount off both long edges.

Follow the Never Fail Miters instructions on pages 54–55 to add the borders to the quilt.

Finishing the Corner Appliqué

Place the border corners on the light box and trace placement lines for the corner appliqué flowers. Finish adding the corner appliqué pieces.

Option: You may want to add birds, butterflies, or dragonflies that escape the quilt center into the border or sashing areas.

Backing

Remove the selvage from the 8½ yards of backing fabric and cut two sections 115" long and one section 58" long. Cut the 58" section in half lengthwise and piece end to end. This will make the center of your backing and will be approximately 20" wide x 115" long. Sew a long section to each side of the center as illustrated.

Binding

You will need ten strips cut 2" wide for 385" of continuous binding.

See the instructions on pages 54–57 for finishing your quilt.

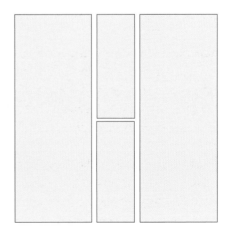

Backing

The Finishing Touch

Never-Fail Miters

Measure the quilt vertically down the center, including the seam allowances. Measure the quilt horizontally through the center including the seam allowances. Make a note of both measurements. **Accurate measurements are critical**.

Vertical measurement of quilt [   ]

Horizontal measurement of quilt [   ]

Border width of quilt [   ]

Determine the width of the border (unfinished). [   ]

Here is the formula for cutting a border that you want to finish with mitered corners:

Border width x2 + Vertical measurement of quilt + 2" = side border length

Border width x2 + Horizontal measurement of quilt + 2" = top and bottom border length

Use this formula and cut border strips for Blossoms of Friendship.

Divide the vertical measurement in half and write it down to refer to.

½ of the vertical measurement = [   ]

½ of the horizontal measurement = [   ]

Measure from the center of the side border strip to this measurement and place a mark in the seam allowance of the **inside** edge of the border. Measure from the center to the opposite end, and place another mark. Double check these measurements to ensure an accurate cut of the mitered corners.

Lay the border on your cutting table with the marked edge toward you. Cut a 45-degree angle starting at the mark you made in the seam allowance and angling outward to the outside edge of the border.

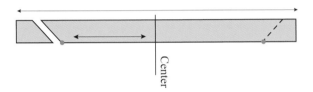

Repeat on the opposite end being sure your angles both go outward. The outside edge of the border is longer at both ends than the inside edge.

Center and pin this border to your quilt body. Sew to your quilt beginning ¼" in from the edge and ending ¼" before the opposite end. Repeat for the second side border.

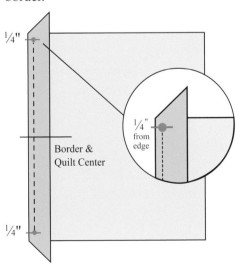

Using the horizontal measurement of the quilt center **before** you added the side borders, repeat the process for the top and bottom borders.

Using a ⅜" seam, pin and sew the corners together on the mitered 45-degree angle. Begin at the outside point and end one stitch short of the seam attaching the border to the quilt. Press away from the side borders and trim seams to ¼".

Batting

Your choice of batting depends on the intended use of the quilt and whether you are hand or machine quilting. We prefer Hobbs® wool or silk batting for hand quilting and cotton for machine quilting.

Layering for Quilting

Press and lay the backing wrong side up. Tape, pin, or clip to a table on all four sides. Be sure not to stretch the backing but keep it flat and slightly taut.

Center the batting on top and hand smooth the creases out. It is helpful to lay polyester batting out flat 48 hours prior to use so the creases will relax. Creases in cotton batting can be smoothed out by hand.

Place the pressed quilt top, right side up, centered on top of the batt. Pin baste for machine quilting or thread baste with large stitches for hand quilting. Baste every 4" to 6" vertically and diagonally to secure the three layers together. Fold the backing to the front just covering the quilt edge to protect the extended batt and baste in place.

Quilting

See the quilting patterns we used on our quilts on page 57.

Binding

Before you add the binding, make sure the edge is straight and the quilting goes to the edge to be bound. If the quilting is not to the edge, you will need to baste the outside edge of the quilt, within the seam allowance, to keep the quilt from pulling or stretching when adding the binding.

We used straight-of-grain binding as all of the quilts have straight-edge borders. Bias binding can be used if you prefer.

Using the 2" binding strips, sew the strips together with 45-degree angle seams. Allow for enough binding for twice the width of the quilt plus twice the length plus 10" extra to allow for the corners. When you have a long enough binding strip, fold in half lengthwise and press.

Beginning near the middle of one side, align the binding raw edges with the raw edge of the quilt top. Leave a 12" tail of the binding extended above where you begin sewing. Begin sewing with a back tack, maintaining an even ¼" seam. **DO NOT STRETCH** or pull on the binding. It is best to use a walking foot. Stop sewing ¼" short of the corner and back tack.

Remove from the machine and fold back the binding away from the quilt on a 45-degree angle.

Refold forward aligning with the next side of the quilt to be sewn. This fold should lie even with the side you just sewed and the raw edge of binding even with the side you are ready to sew.

Begin sewing your next side right on this last fold and sew to the next corner.

When you are around the quilt and about 18" from where you started, back tack and remove the quilt from the machine.

Take the two binding tails hanging loose from each end and bring them together where you want them to connect. Fold the excess tails back away from each other and finger press well on each fold.

Open out the right binding tail and lay it vertically, right side up. Open the left tail out and place it right side down with the finger-pressed fold to the left of the right tail.

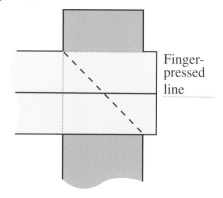

Finger-pressed line

Quilting Patterns

Corner Quilting

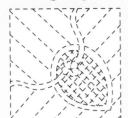

Border: Every ⅜" from center to corner quilting pattern

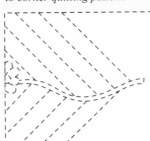

(*Outline appliqué then every ¼" up to appliqué*)

Block Background Quilting Pattern

Corner Block Quilting Pattern

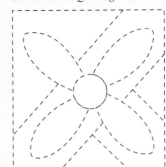

Inside Lattice Quilting Pattern

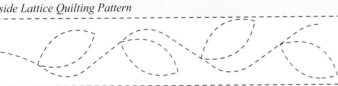

Outside Lattice Quilting Pattern

⅜" Squares on-point

This will form a square in the tails. Pin together. Draw a 45-degree line from the top left to the bottom right of this square and sew on this line. Remove pins and refold the binding, checking to be sure you have not twisted the tails and that the binding fits the quilt. Trim the seam to ¼" and finger press open. Pin the completed binding to fit the opening on the quilt and finish stitching.

Trim around the quilt, leaving plenty of batting and backing to completely fill the quilt binding.

Roll the binding to the back and blind stitch down over the row of machine stitching from the front. The corner miters will already be stitched in on the front. Fold the miter in the opposite direction on the back and tack before you continue sewing the next side.

Labeling

Make a label for the back of the quilt. This label should be written in permanent ink so the quilt can be identified. Heat-set the ink on the label by using a hot iron, without steam. Include all desired information, but the minimum should be the name of the quilt, maker's name, city and state, date, name of the pattern/book/magazine and publisher.

Hanging Sleeve

Make a sleeve for the back of your quilt. It will protect your quilt from damage caused by pinning, clamping, etc., when hanging it for display.

Cut fabric as long as the width of the quilt and 10½" wide. Make a double ¾" hem in each end. With the right side of the fabric to the outside, butt the raw edges together, forming a tube. Press well. Refold the tube, wrong sides together and raw edges even, and stitch with a ¼" seam. Press this seam open so that it will lie flat against the quilt backing.

Hand stitch the tube on the creased folds, centered on the quilt and ½" below the top binding. Make certain not to go through to the front of your quilt. By stitching on the pressed folds, you have allowed for the thickness of a hanging rod and assured that the quilt will lie flat from the front side. You may re-press the sleeve flat against the back of your quilt.

Aunt Fannie's Fantasy

Sometime around 1942, my father took his young family to live on Aunt Fannie's farm. She was a widowed dry land farmer in south Texas near Hondo. She needed help on the farm and we needed a place to live while Dad went to an electrical trade school, so we lived there rent free.

It wasn't much of a farm as all she raised were cotton, a few cows, and chickens. I remember being afraid of tarantulas, rattlesnakes, and the javelinas that roamed around during the night.

When it came time to harvest the cotton and I heard my brother Tom was going to help pick, I pestered my mom to let me pick, too. So she made me a little "cotton-pickin" bag suitable for my size as I was only four years old. It wasn't long until the novelty wore off and the hot sun got to me, so I spent the rest of the afternoon asleep on the bags of cotton.

I remember how Aunt Fannie loved flowers and tried so hard to grow a few in coffee cans on her back porch, but they never amounted to much due to the lack of good dirt and water. That's how I came to name this quilt AUNT FANNIE'S FANTASY.

Barbara

AUNT FANNIE'S FANTASY

*Quilt size: 35" x 39". Made and hand quilted by Mary Ross and
machine quilted by Joyce Schiltz, both of Montrose, Colorado.*

Mary Ross & Barbara Scheu ~ Delightful Quilts in Bloom

Yardage

Background ~ ⅞ yard
Border ~ 1¼ yards
Appliqué ~ scraps or sweet 16s
Bias trim ~ ½ yard
Backing ~ 1¼ yards
Binding ~ ¼ yard
Batting ~ 39" x 43"

Cutting

Background block
    27" x 31"rectangle

Construction

See the General Directions for Appliqué on pages
10–11 for alignment and pattern-transfer instructions.

Appliqué Sequence
1–120

Press the appliqué block but do not trim.

Shaped Border

To make the border pattern, draw a 24" x 28" rectangle
on tracing or freezer paper. Make a corner template
(page 64) and trace the curved line onto the four
corners of the rectangle. Cut out around the rectangle
and along the curved corners. Fold the pattern in half
horizontally and vertically to make center guidelines.

Center the pattern over the right side of the appliqué
block, pin in place, and trace around it with a fine line
pencil.

For a seamless border, cut a rectangle of the border
fabric 35" x 39". Press in center vertical and horizontal
lines. Remove the border pattern from the appliqué and
align with pressed center fold lines. Trace around the
pattern using the same fine line pencil.

Cut out the border on the drawn line **without cutting into the outside border area. Make a small snip in the center area** but close to the pencil line to get started, and then cut right on the drawn line. Be careful not to stretch this fabric.

Lay the border on top of the appliqué block, right sides of both facing up, butting the cut edge to the drawn line on the appliqué block. Pin in place.

Zigzag stitch through both layers, close to the raw edge on the border fabric with an extended, loose stitch, using your walking foot. If you do not have a walking foot, then hand baste the layers together before sewing. With the block right-side down and on a flat surface, carefully trim away the excess background fabric of the block to within ¼" of the overlapped seams.

Prepare 120" of bias trim. Cut bias strips 1⅛" wide, seam end-to-end with 45-degree angle seams, and tri-fold as shown in the General Directions for Bias Stems (page 9).

Appliqué the bias trim to the border, covering the inside raw edge of the border fabric. Begin by leaving about 5" of bias hanging loose. When you are within 10 inches of closing the bias, stop and open the beginning tail flat, face up. Open the ending tail face up and lay it on the top of the beginning tail. Be sure the 45-degree angle of the beginning tail is covered by a full ½" and cut the ending tail on a 45-degree angle in the same direction as the beginning tail. Place the tails right sides together and hand stitch a ¼" seam. Finger press this seam open and refold the bias. Pin in place and finish appliquéing down on both sides.

Make 160" of binding cut 2" wide. See the instructions on pages 54–57 for finishing your quilt.

Mary Ross & Barbara Scheu ~ Delightful Quilts in Bloom

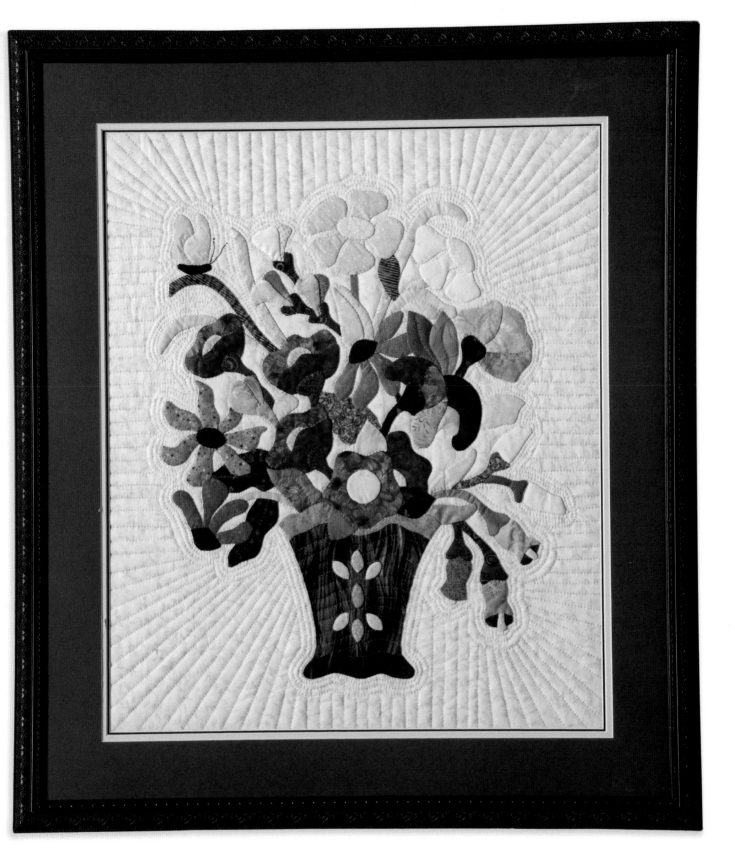

Aunt Fannie's Fantasy

Made and hand quilted by Peggy Maynes, Montrose, Colorado.
*Peggy's AUNT FANNIE'S FANTASY was hand quilted and professionally framed. She chose to
leave it rectangular and use the framing for the border.*

Aunt Fannie's Fantasy

Enlarge Illustration by 200%

Mary Ross & Barbara Scheu ~ Delightful Quilts in Bloom

Aunt Fannie's Fantasy

Enlarge Illustration by 200%

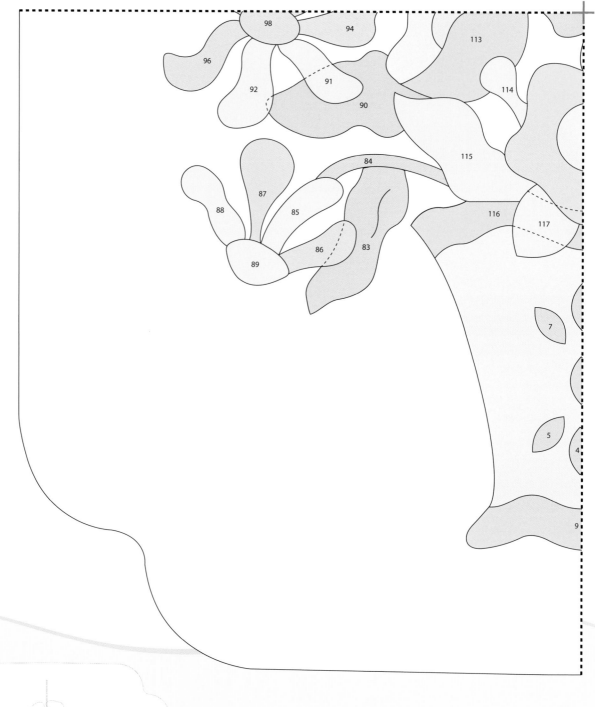

Aunt Fannie's Fantasy

Enlarge Illustration by 200%

Mary Ross & Barbara Scheu ~ Delightful Quilts in Bloom

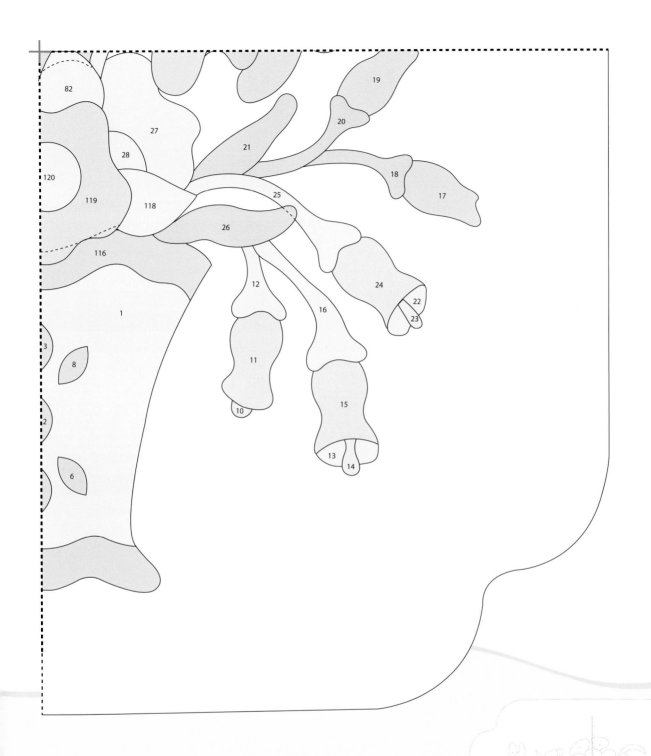

Aunt Fannie's Fantasy

Enlarge Illustration by 200%

Mary Ross & Barbara Scheu ~ Delightful Quilts in Bloom

Mary Ross & Barbara Scheu ~ Delightful Quilts in Bloom

GRAND POPPY

William H. Callahan, born in 1873, was my maternal grandfather. His nickname was Bid, or Shorty to some. I do not know why he was called Bid, but I know there were a lot of farm auctions in our area and I suspect it would have had something to do with that. His favorite evening snack was cornbread soaked in buttermilk.

Grandpa liked to tease my sister and me. Whenever he would come to visit and find our nails painted, he wanted to know if our fingers were bleeding. We laughed a lot with Grandpa, but we always respected him for his grand manner and way of life. Grandpa belonged to the Friends faith and we heard stories of his getting out in the heavy wet snowstorms to hitch the horses to the wagon so that members of the congregation made it to church.

His friends always asked him, "How tall are you, Shorty?" and his answer was always, "Oh, not very tall at all, just 5 feet 18½ inches." Yes, we looked up to Grandpa in more ways than one. He really was a Grand Poppy!
Mary

GRAND POPPY

Quilt size: 23" x 28". Made by Mary Ross and machine quilted by Joyce Schiltz, both of Montrose, Colorado. Our design of this GRAND POPPY wallhanging was the inspiration for Barbara's watercolor painting.

Yardage

Background ~ ½ yard

Flower ~ Sweet 16s or scraps measuring up
to 11" square
Leaves ~ Scraps or sweet 16s
Border ~ ⅝ yard
Fringe ~ 1½" x 9"
Backing ~ ¾ yard
Binding ~ ¼ yard
Batting ~ 27" x 32"

Cutting

Background
    15½" x 20½" rectangle
Borders
    2 strips 5" x 20½"
    2 strips 5" x 24½"
Binding
    3 strips 2" x 40"

Construction

Add the 5" x 20½" border strips to the top and bottom
of the background. Press the seam allowance toward
the border strips.

Add the 5" x 24½" border strips to the sides of the
background. Press the seam allowance toward the
border strips.

OR you can choose to miter the corners. See the
Never-Fail Miters instructions on pages 54–55.

See the General Directions for Appliqué on pages
10–11 for alignment and pattern transfer instructions.

Mary Ross & Barbara Scheu ~ Delightful Quilts in Bloom

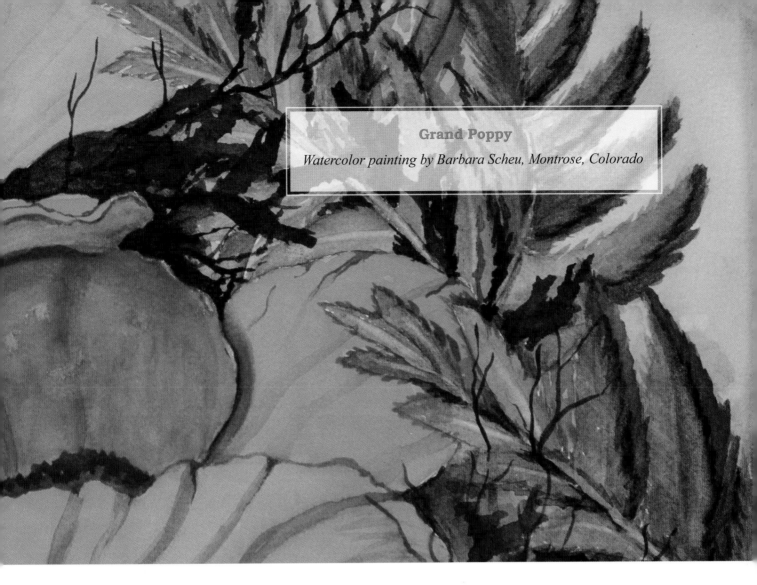

Grand Poppy

Watercolor painting by Barbara Scheu, Montrose, Colorado

Appliqué Sequence
1 – 23

Tuck 24 and 25 under stem 26 and appliqué only to the asterisks shown on the pattern.

26 – 29

Clip the 30 seam allowance only at the asterisk, almost to the pattern edge, so the seam will lie flat under 32. Prepare piece number 31. Pieces 31A, 31B, and 31C are sunshine or shadow pieces that are optional. Your fabric may not need this preparation.

Iron the freezer-paper pattern onto the wrong side of the fabric for piece 31 and add seam allowance all around. Remove the freezer paper and save for later. Align and appliqué pieces 31A– 31C to piece 31.

Draw the 31D oval on the right side of piece 31 fabric. Stitch the fringe around the oval with the seam allowance of the fringe inside the oval or stitch the fringe in a horseshoe shape over the top of the oval with a small bar of fringe across the bottom with the fringe heading toward the oval. This lower bar of fringe seam allowance will tuck under piece 32. Add 31D on top of the fringe seams. Press the completed piece 31 on the back again and continue appliquéing.

31–33

Press the finished appliqué and trim the borders to 4½" wide.

Join the binding strips with a bias seam.

See the instructions on pages 54–57 for finishing your quilt.

Grand Poppy

Enlarge Illustration by 200%

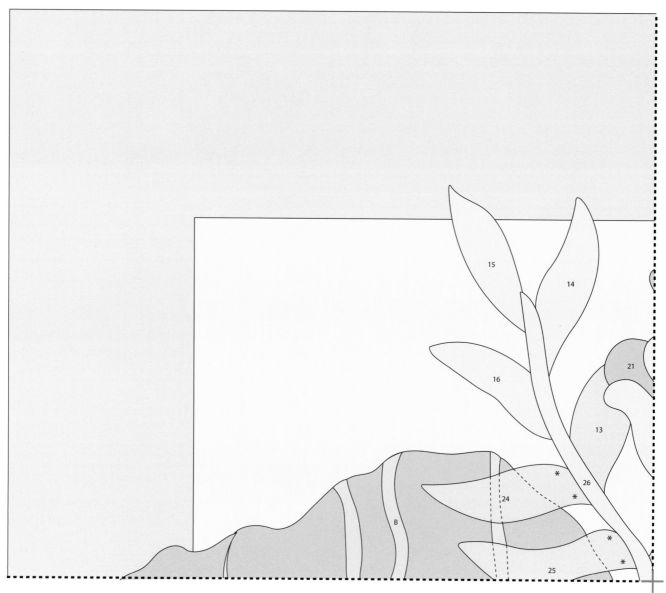

Mary Ross & Barbara Scheu ~ Delightful Quilts in Bloom

Grand Poppy

Enlarge Illustration by 200%

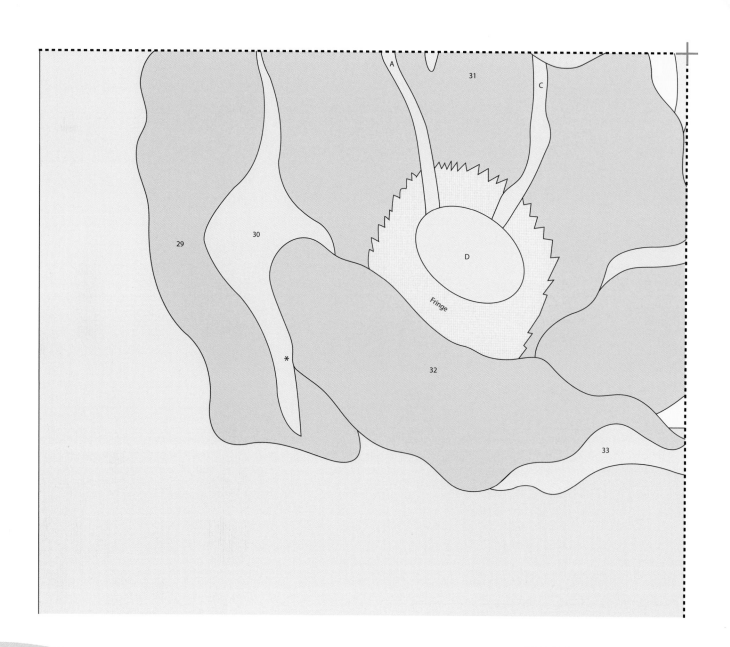

Grand Poppy

Enlarge Illustration by 200%

Mary Ross & Barbara Scheu ~ Delightful Quilts in Bloom

Grand Poppy

Enlarge Illustration by 200%

Daisy Dew

Yardage

Background ~ ⅝ yard
Appliqué ~ Scraps that coordinate
  with the border fabrics
Inside border ~ ⅛ yard
Outside border ~ ⅝ yard
Backing ~ ⅞ yard
Batting ~ 29" x 35"
Binding ~ ¼ yard

Cutting

Background
  one 17" x 22" rectangle
Inside border
  4 strips 1" x 40"
Outside border
  3 strips 5" x 40"
Binding
  3 strips 2" x 40"

Construction

See the General Directions for Appliqué on pages 10–11
for alignment and pattern-transfer instructions.

Appliqué Sequence
1 – 30

Use a black embroidered stem stitch for the bleeding heart
stems or mark with a permanent fabric and heat set.

See the instructions on pages 54–57 for finishing
your quilt.

DAISY DEW

Quilt size: 25" x 31". Finished block size: 16" x 20".

A Cardinal's View

Yardage

Background ~ ⅝ yard
Scraps for appliqué that
   coordinate with the border fabrics
Inside border ~ ⅛ yard
Outside border ~ ⅝ yard
Backing ~ ⅞ yard
Batting ~ 29" x 35"
Binding ~ ¼ yard

Cutting

Background
   one 17" x 22" rectangle
Inside border
   4 strips 1" x 40"
Outside border
   3 strips 5" x 40"
Binding
   3 strips 2" x 40"

Construction

See the General Directions for Appliqué on pages
10–11 for alignment and pattern-transfer instructions.

Appliqué Sequence
1 – 9

Appliqué number 1 to background.
Appliqué 2 onto 3 and baste the 2/3 unit in place on
the background.

To prepare piece 4 for reverse appliqué, draw the full
circle of the birdhouse door on the right side of the
fabric. Draw another circle approximately ³⁄₁₆" inside
the first. Cut out the inner circle and clip around the
³⁄₁₆" seam allowance, being careful not to clip into the
outer circle.
Machine stitch 4–7 together.
Machine stitch 8–9 together.
Align 4–7 unit over 2–3 and reverse appliqué the
birdhouse door.
Appliqué the outside edges of 6, 4, and 7.
Appliqué the 8–9 roof.

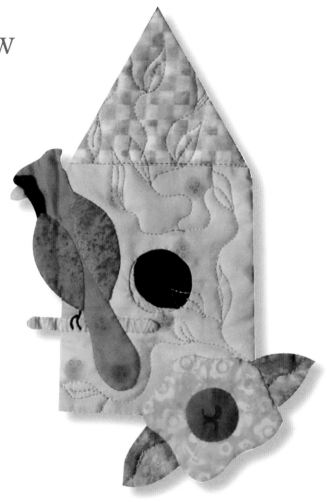

10 – 41

After appliqué is completed, press the block. Trim to
16 ½" x 21½", making sure your appliqué is centered
and level with the bottom edge.

Measure the width of the block through the center
and cut two strips that length from the 1" inner border
strips. Sew them to the top and bottom of the block.
Press the seam allowances away from the block.

Measure the length of the block through the center
and cut two strips that length from the 1" inner border
strips. Sew them to the sides of the block. Press the
seam allowances away from the block.

In the same manner, measure and cut the 5" outer
border strips, and add them to the quilt.

See the instructions on pages 54–57 for finishing
your quilt.

A CARDINAL'S VIEW

Quilt size: 25" x 31". Finished block size: 16" x 20".

Mary Ross & Barbara Scheu ~ Delightful Quilts in Bloom

Mary Ross & Barbara Scheu ~ Delightful Quilts in Bloom

Daisy Dew

Enlarge Illustration by 200%

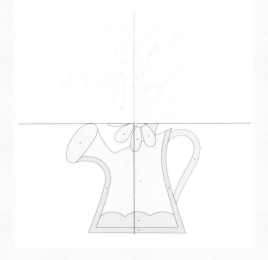

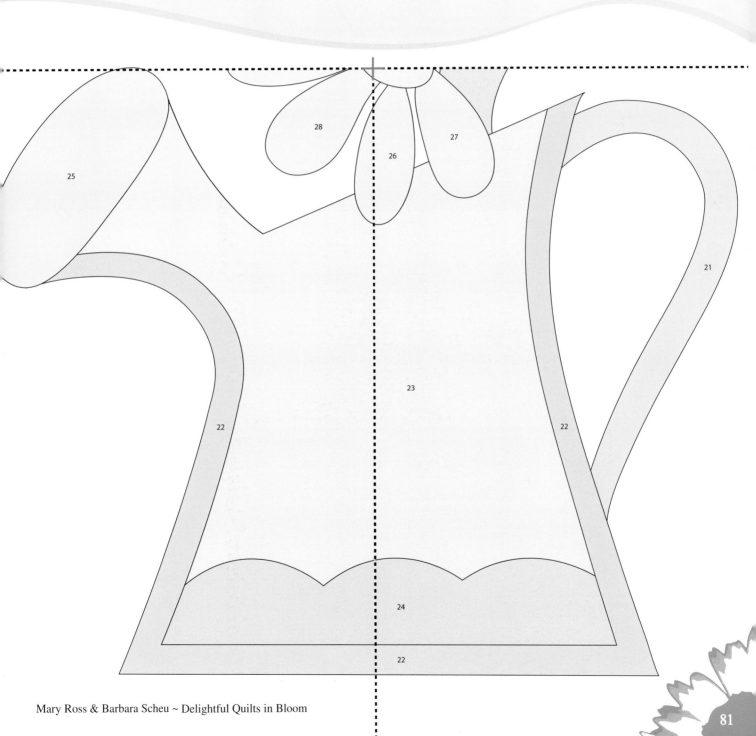

25

28

26

27

21

23

22

22

24

22

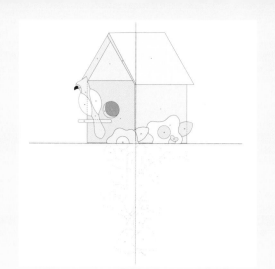

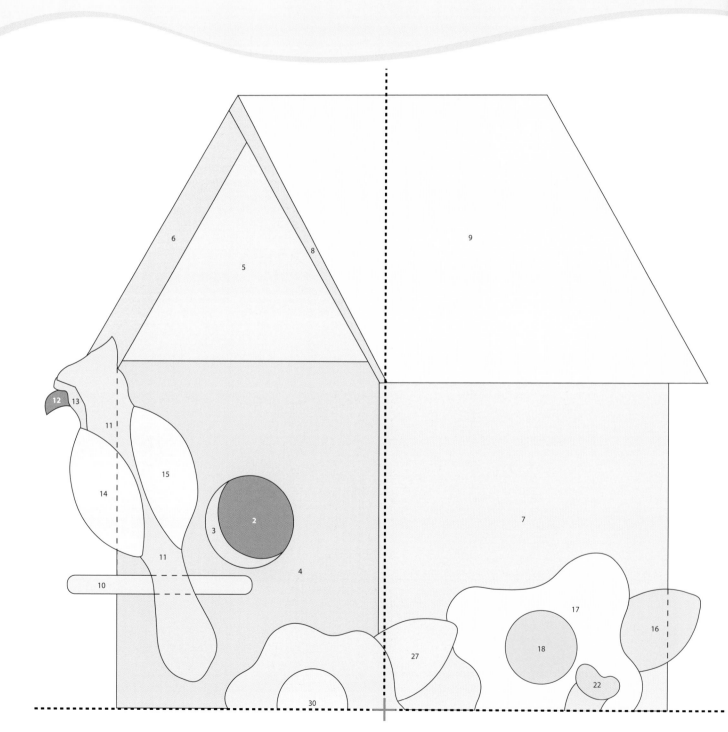

Mary Ross & Barbara Scheu ~ Delightful Quilts in Bloom

A Cardinal's View

Enlarge Illustration by 200%

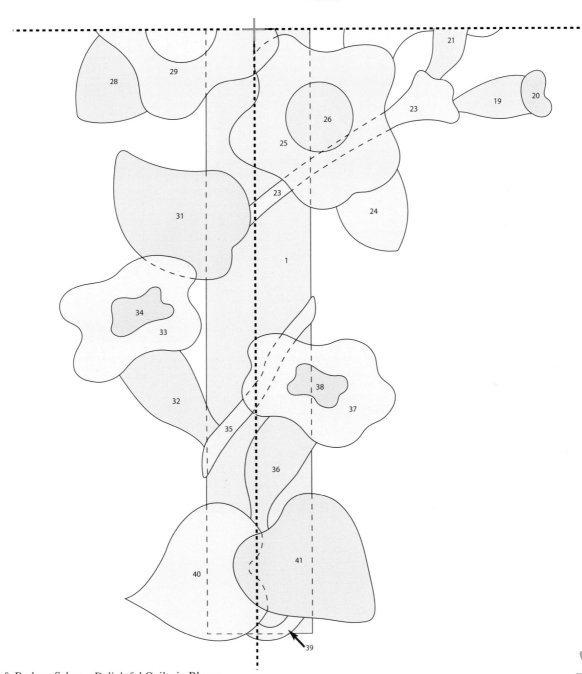

HIGH SOCIETY
Quilt size: 27" x 36". Finished block size 7" x 16".
Made by Mary Ross and machine quilted by Laurie Gerse, both of Montrose, Colorado.

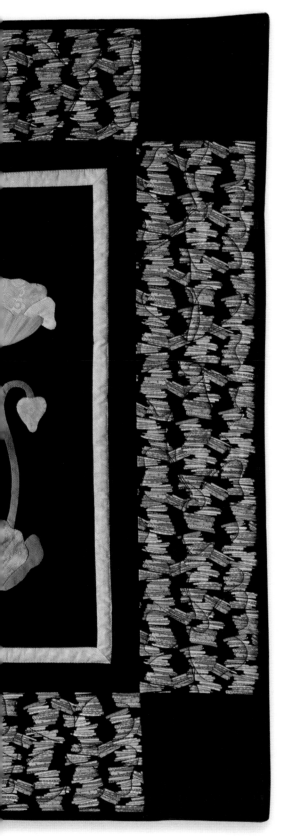

HIGH SOCIETY

Yardage

Background, sashing, & cornerstones ~ ¾ yard
Three inside borders ~ ⅛ yard each
Appliqué ~ ¼ yard scraps
Border ~ ⅝ yard   Binding ~ ¼ yard
Backing ~ ¾ yard   Batting ~ 31" x 40"

Cutting

Background
    3 rectangles 8" x 17"
    4 strips 1½" x 17½"
    2 strips 1½" x 28½"
    Four 4½" x 4½" squares
Inside borders
    2 strips 1" x 7½" of each fabric
    2 strips 1" x 17½" of each fabric

Border
    2 strips 4½" x 28½"
    2 strips 4½" x 19½"
Binding
    4 strips 2" x 40"

Construction

See the General Directions for Appliqué on pages 10–11 for alignment and pattern-transfer instructions. Appliqué the three flowers onto the background rectangles.

Press and trim each block to measure 7½" x 16½", making sure the flowers are square to the bottom and centered on your block.

Sew a 1" x 7½" inside border strip to the top and bottom of each block. Press the seam allowances away from the block.

Sew a 1" x 17½" inside border strip each side of the three blocks. Press the seam allowances away from the block.

Measure the length of the blocks and trim them to the same size if necessary. Cut four 1½" sashing strips the length of the blocks. Arrange the three blocks in a row and add the sashing strips as shown. Press the seam allowances toward the sashing.

Measure the width of the block and sashing unit through the center. Cut two 1½" strips to that measurement and add to the top and bottom. Press the seam allowances toward the sashing.

Borders

Sew the 4½" x 28½" borders to the top and bottom of the quilt. Press the seam allowances away from the blocks.

Sew a 4½" cornerstone to each end of the 4½" x 19½" border strips. Press the seam allowances toward the corner blocks. Sew these borders to each side of the quilt. See the instructions on pages 54–57 for finishing your quilt.

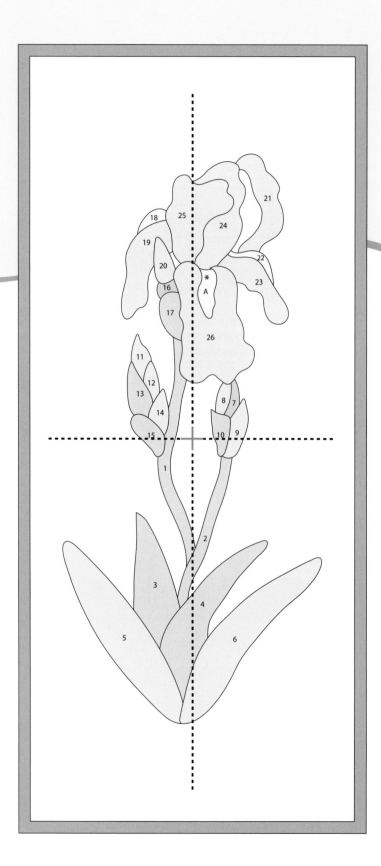

High Society

Enlarge Illustration by 200%

Appliqué sequence:
- 1–25
- Add A to 26
- 26

High Society

Enlarge Illustration by 200%

Appliqué sequence:

- 1–15

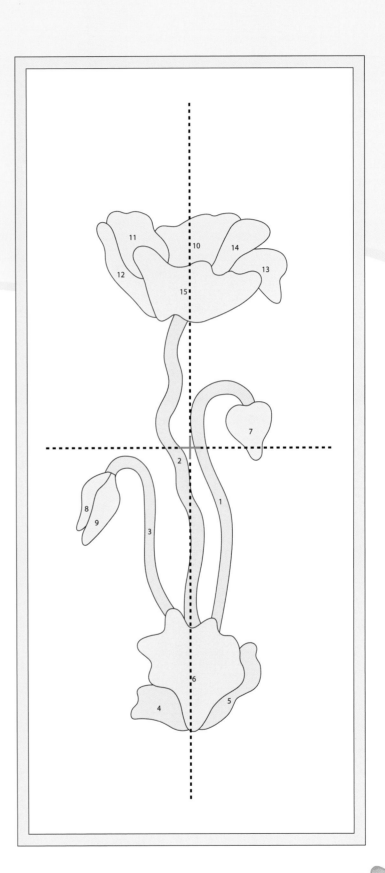

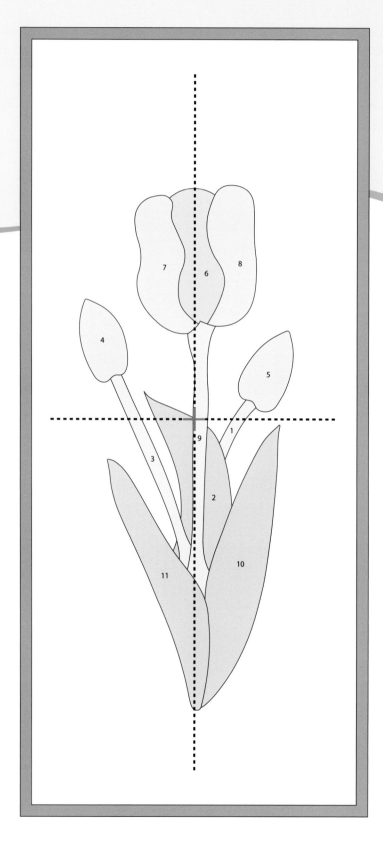

Enlarge Illustration by 200%

Appliqué sequence:
• 1–11

Mary Ross & Barbara Scheu ~ Delightful Quilts in Bloom

COLUMBINE RUN THROUGH IT

One week every summer I was allowed to go to my Uncle Jess and Aunt Maudie's farm. Their boys were grown, so I would get lots of attention. The purpose of my visit was a new outfit for school. Maudie would have a pattern already picked out and I was there for the fittings.

Between fittings, I was able to play with the animals and work in the garden. I gleaned many memories from that garden, but my favorite was picking blackberries. That was my favorite job as I would eat more than went into the basket, but I always saved enough for the pie that would appear on the table that night.

Sometimes Aunt Maudie would run out of feed sack fabric for my dress, and Uncle Jess would be dispatched to the feed store with a swatch of the fabric to buy another bag of feed.

Today Barb brings her farm stories from Texas and I bring mine from Indiana but we now enjoy our Colorado. For our table runner, we chose columbine, which run through our mountain meadows and fill the hills with color.

The table runner was inspired by the watercolor of the same name, painted by Barbara.

Mary

COLUMBINE RUN THROUGH IT

Watercolor painting by Barbara Scheu, Montrose, Colorado

Yardage

Background and backing ~ ½ yard
Border and binding ~ ¾ yard
Appliqué ~ assorted scraps
Batting ~ 24" x 50"

Cutting

Background 15½" x 45" rectangle
Binding
    4 strips 2" x 40"

Construction

See the General Directions for Appliqué on pages 10–11 for alignment and pattern-transfer instructions.

COLUMBINE RUN THROUGH IT Table Runner

*Quilt size: 18" x 43½". Made by Ludene Smith and machine
quilted by Joyce Schiltz, both of Montrose, Colorado.*

Appliqué sequence
1 – 133
Pieces 133–137 need to have a perfect ¼" seam
allowance added to the straight edge sides.

Press and trim the appliquéd background to
14½" x 44".

Align pieces 133–137 with the corners of the trimmed
background and appliqué the curved edge in place.
Carefully cut away the background behind these pieces
as they are now your new corners.

You may choose to add machine or hand embroidery,
inking, or other embellishment to enhance the centers
of your columbine.

See the Never-Fail Miters instructions on page 54 or
cut 2 strips 2½" x 44" and sew them to the long sides
of the runner. Cut 2 strips 2½" x 18½" and sew them
to each end.

See the Finishing Touch (pages 55–57) for instructions
on layering and binding your runner.

Mary Ross & Barbara Scheu ~ Delightful Quilts in Bloom

Mary Ross & Barbara Scheu ~ Delightful Quilts in Bloom

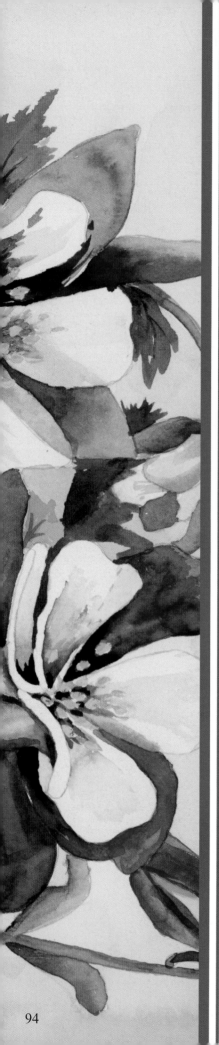

About the Authors

Mary Ross, with her years of experience in quilting techniques, and Barbara Scheu, with expertise in painting and artwork, have joined forces to share in creating the appliqué blocks, borders, and projects for this book.

Mary Ross

Mary was born in Indiana, moved to Colorado Springs in 1963, and retired to Montrose, Colorado, with her husband, Pete, in 1995. She gives of her time to serve her church, her family, and keeps active in her local guilds. She also enjoys the outdoors, making time to hike, camp, and travel with Pete.

Mary has taught classes, lectured, and demonstrated quilting around the Midwest. She enjoys hand quilting the most but delights in all forms of the art of quilting. She began quilting in 1979 and prefers the more traditional designs. She still remembers her grandmother hand piecing many quilts from flour sacks and dress scraps.

Mary has had quilt patterns published and has won many awards in local and state quilt shows. A request to design appliqué for a block-of-the-month program resulted in the creation of the many projects in this book.

Barbara Scheu

Barbara Scheu was born in Texas, raised in Montana, and has lived in Colorado for the last 49 years with her husband, Jim.

Barb's creativity showed up early. She learned to sew on a treadle machine at the tender age of 10. She made her school clothes and learned to knit, crochet, and embroider. She has always loved to draw and began taking art classes in high school. She began painting in earnest in 1990 when she joined the Montrose Visual Arts Guild. Barbara has won numerous awards in art shows, taught classes, and sold her paintings. She considers herself self-taught but continues to take classes and workshops to improve her gift.

In 2003, Mary, whose work Barb admired, was giving a demonstration at a local quilt club. Inspired, she joined the club and began making quilts herself. Although it has been just four years, she has already won awards in quilting. She won third place for her wearable art and recently won three first-place ribbons and Grand Champion for her design of a wildlife quilt. She believes that when she chose a mentor, she chose the best—her friend, Mary Ross.

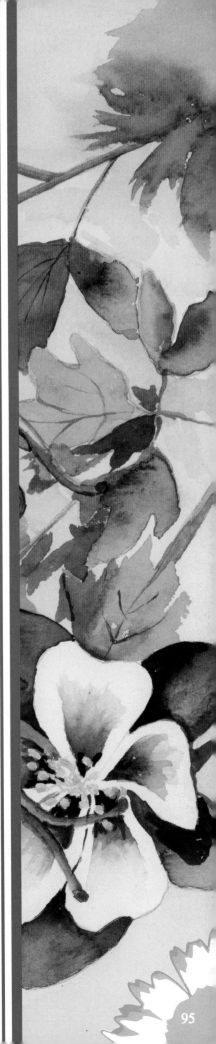

More AQS Books

This is only a small selection of the books available from the American Quilter's Society. AQS books are known world-wide for timely topics, clear writing, beautiful color photos, and accurate illustrations and patterns. The following books are available from your local bookseller, quilt shop, or public library.

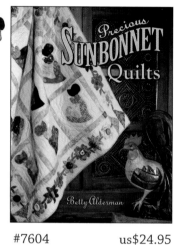

#7604   us$24.95

#7605   us$24.95

#7600   us$26.95

#7012   us$19.95

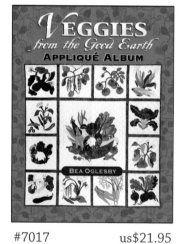

#7017   us$21.95

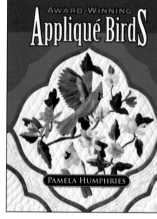

#7494   us$21.95

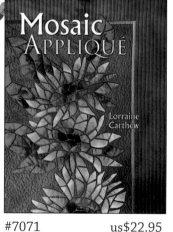

#7071   us$22.95

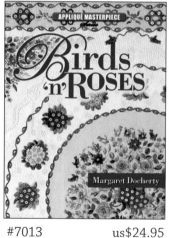

#7013   us$24.95

#7486   us$22.95